ROCK
POINT

A division of the Quarto Publishing Group USA Inc.
276 Fifth Avenue Suite 206
New York, New York 10001

ROCK POINT and the distinctive Rock Point logo are
trademarks of the Quarto Publishing Group USA Inc.

© 2014 text by Harriet Ziefert, Inc.
© 2014 illustrations by Chuck Nitzberg

This 2014 edition published by Rock Point
by arrangement with Harriet Ziefert, Inc.

ISBN-13: 978-1-6310-6012-0

Printed in China

2 4 6 8 10 9 7 5 3 1

www.rockpointpub.com

Little Miseries

NEW YORK

Illustrations by Chuck Nitzberg

Little Miseries
NEW YORK

WINTER

Misery

is digging your car out after the snowplows have buried it.

Misery is waiting
for the snowplows
anywhere other
than in Midtown.

Misery is when the snow
in front of one building
on your block
hasn't been shoveled.

Misery
is dirty snow!

Misery
is walking your dog after
the sidewalk has been salted.

Misery
is trying to take a picture
at Rockefeller Center
without including
multiple strangers.

Misery
is a cold
subway
platform.

Misery is the wind between the tall buildings.

Misery
is sweating
under your coat
when riding on
public transportation.

Misery
is too much heat
in your tiny apartment.

Misery is a MetroCard machine that only takes cash.

Misery is that guy who wants a free swipe from your MetroCard.

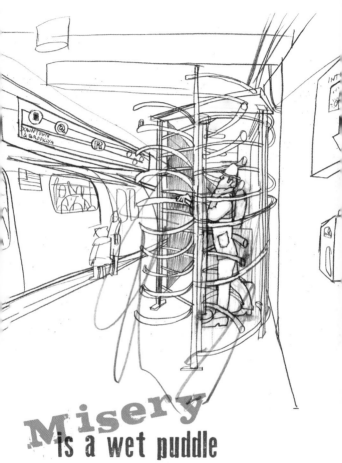

Misery is a wet puddle on the subway seat.

Misery is trying to catch a cab on New Year's Eve.

Misery is trying to catch a cab when it's snowing.

Misery is when your whole family can't fit into your apartment for holiday dinner.

Misery is trying to come up with a story for kids who ask, "Why is there a Santa on every corner?"

Misery is stepping over pools
of ugly gray slush
at every street corner.

Misery is trying to find a restaurant
for New Year's Eve
without a prix fixe menu
that comes close to
the price of a small car...

and forget about
Valentine's Day!

SPRING

Misery is MoMA on the weekends.

Misery
is driving behind
a horse-drawn carriage
on its way
to Central Park.

Misery is getting stuck
behind a sanitation truck
on a side street.

Misery is being asked
for spare change
when dining outdoors.

Misery
is going to Central Park
on the perfect
spring day...
and the rest of the city
has the same idea.

Misery
is people who pronounce
Houston Street
as if it were
a city in Texas.

Misery

is arriving 30 seconds late
to feed the meter...
and the traffic cop refuses
to stop writing the ticket,
because he's already started.

Misery
is missing your stop
on an express bus,
and the next stop
is 15 blocks away.

Misery

is trying to understand the announcements on the subway

Misery

is when the person next to you falls asleep on your shoulder... and drools.

Misery

is getting the "please swipe again" message while you watch the train leave the station.

Misery
is pigeon poop dropping
out of the sky onto
your shoulder
or your head.

Misery
is the $75.00
charge for the
first hour
in a parking lot.

Misery
is dog owners who
never "curb their dogs."

Misery
is alternate-side-
of-the-street parking.

Misery
is looking for
a parking space.

Misery

is coming up from the subway to find that it's pouring, and you don't have an umbrella.

Misery

is the $5 umbrella
that you just bought
on the street falling apart
in the wind.

Misery
is when a cab insanely
crosses three lanes of
traffic to pick you up.

Misery
is finding the perfect
parking space blocked
by a mountain
of garbage bags.

Misery

is the bicyclist who rides in the wrong direction in the bike lane.

Misery

is waitng on a line that goes around the block for:

brunch...

a movie...

a sale...

tickets...

renewing your driver's license...

a cupcake?

SUMMER

Misery
is a two-hour subway ride to get home from the beach.

Misery

is when your "backyard" is a fire escape.

Misery is an $8 beer at Yankee Stadium.

Misery is being a Mets fan.

Misery

is being handed a flyer
even after you've
politely declined,
then not being able
to find a garbage can
to throw it away.

Misery

is a pile of take-out menus in front of your door.

Misery
is garbage collection day
when the temperature
is over 80 degrees.

Misery

is a brownout and the accompanying fear that the power might go out altogether.

Misery

is when everyone leaves to go to the beach for the weekend, and you're stuck in the city with the tourists.

Misery

is the smell of hot meat wafting from food carts.

Misery
is a car radio
at full blast
at 1 am.

Misery
is really inappropriate
clothing in public spaces.

Misery
is getting doused
by kids playing
at an open fire hydrant.

Misery
is that subway car
with no air conditioning.

Misery
is the smell.

Misery
is a mariachi band in your car.

Misery
is the ferry during bad weather.

Misery

is waiting for the subway
on the steamy platform,
and then shivering
in the air-conditioned
subway car.

Misery

is getting on the bus with
not enough money on your
MetroCard, and no change.

Misery

is a different
service change
every weekend
on the subway
due to ongoing
construction.

Misery is not being able to turn off the video in the back of the cab.

Misery is the smell of your cab driver's lunch.

Misery
is the window in the cab that won't open.

Misery
is the window in the cab that won't close.

Misery

is a loud block party.

Misery
is a different
street closure
every weekend
because of street fairs.

Misery
is tourists.

Misery

is walking behind a group of tourists while trying to get to work.

Misery
Is the hot asphalt sticking to the bottom of your sneakers.

Misery
is humidity,
humidity,
humidity.

Misery is cherry bombs on the night of July 4th.

Misery is trying to find a spot where you can actually see the fireworks, without being trampled.

Misery

is summer
in New York City.
Period.

NEW YORK

Misery

is when your Thanksgiving turkey is bigger than your oven.

Misery
is having to get up at
the crack of dawn to nab
a decent spot for viewing
the Thanksgiving Day parade...

and then your kids refusing
to stay for more
than 10 minutes because...
"We're cold. Can we go now?"

Misery
is the cost of tolls on all the bridges and tunnels.

Misery

is planning to ride
a Citi Bike
and finding an
empty rack.

Misery is going to
the Museum
of Natural History
the same day
as a group
of 60 first graders.

Misery is not being able to sleep in the city that never sleeps... because of the noise from the never-ending sirens.

Misery
is having to ask
a restaurant if you can use
their bathroom without
ordering anything.

Misery
is waiting for a bathroom
at Starbucks when you
need to go...REALLY bad!

Misery

is an out-of-town friend
who wants to visit Times Square.
And the Empire State Building!
And the Statue of Liberty!

Misery

is having to call
for a reservation
at a restaurant
a month in advance...

and getting attitude
from the maître d´
on the phone.

Misery

is being so close
to the people next
to you at a restaurant
that you can hear
every word...

and their conversation
is more interesting than
the one you are having.

Misery is the $4 price for a bottle of water in Washington Square Park.

Misery is buying it anyway.

Misery

is being given a daisy
by a Hare Krishna.

Misery is New York cab drivers.

Misery is New York drivers.

Misery is out-of-town drivers.

Misery is New York pedestrians.

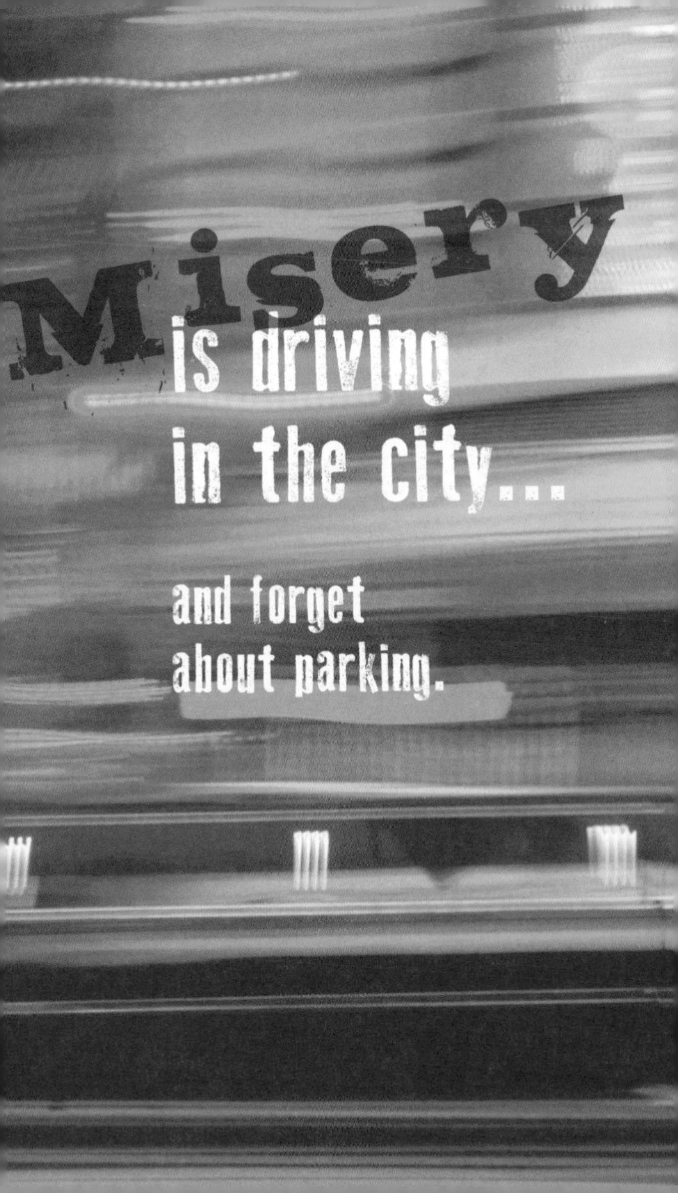
Misery
is driving
in the city...
and forget
about parking.

Happiness

is living in the greatest city in the world.

It's the city that never sleeps,
and why would you want it to?

It's a maddening concrete jungle,
and real New Yorkers wouldn't have it
any other way.

We love you,

BIG APPLE!